Air Fryer Cookbook for Beginners

Easy, Healthy and Delicious Recipes for Your Air Fryer

Savannah Gibbs

Table of Contents

CHAPTER EIGHT

CHAPTER NINE

CHAPTER ONE

Introduction to the Air Fryer

What Is an Air Fryer?

The air fryer was invented in 2010 by the Philips Electronics Company as an alternative to deep frying food. Over the years, this appliance has become a staple in today's kitchen, providing a new and healthy way of preparing food. You may have watched numerous advertisements for the air fryer and probably wondered how it works. If you associate an air fryer with a lot of hot air, then you have the right idea.

An air fryer uses Rapid Air technology to cook foods with little or no oil. Foods are placed in the fryer's basket, and hot air is circulated rapidly around the ingredients. The air helps to heat the food from all sides at once, which is exactly what happens when you deep fry foods using oil. The air fryer uses 90 percent less oil, and won't leave your kitchen with a greasy smell. This technology also ensures an optimal temperature is maintained within the fryer to avoid burning your food. The air fryer will make your food crispy on the outside and tender and tasty on the inside!

Benefits of Air Fryers

When you look at a new kitchen appliance, you want to know the benefits of using it before splurging on the purchase. Let's look at a few benefits of the air fryer, which may give you a clearer idea as to whether or not you should consider getting it for your kitchen.

Healthy

The biggest benefit of using an air fryer to cook food is the obvious health benefits when compared to cooking with a deep fryer. Less oil means less fat and calories, so cutting down the amount of oil you cook with will help make your food healthier.

Faster

An air fryer heats up faster and cooks faster than a traditional oven. In general, it reduces cook times by about 20%. Considering it does not really need any monitoring while you are cooking with it, time is also freed up to focus on other aspects of your daily activities.

Simple to Use

This is an appliance that a person with little to no cooking experience can use. There aren't a lot of buttons on the air fryer to confuse you. All you will need to do is put the ingredients in the basket and set the temperature and the timer without worrying about another thing–the machine will do the rest of the work. There are some fryers that come with additional buttons to indicate what kind of ingredient is being cooked, making it easier for you.

Safe

This appliance is safe to use. It automatically turns off when the food finishes cooking, which prevents overheating the appliance and the food from being burnt. Your children can also use this appliance–you do not have to worry about them burning themselves when cooking since the fryer is essentially oil-free and covered.

Easy to Clean

As food is cooked inside the chamber of air fryer, you won't have oil vapor deposits on the walls, floors, or countertops. All the parts of the air fryer can be removed easily and are dishwasher friendly. If you do not own a dishwasher, you can soak the parts in water and clean them with a sponge, which is easier than having to clean multiple utensils you may have to use when cooking with oil.

Tips for Air Frying

When you use an air fryer for the first time, you may make a few mistakes that could eventually ruin the appliance. Here are a few tips to keep in mind when you start using an air fryer.

Always Shake and Mix

When you cook using oil, it helps to mix your food properly, which cooks every little piece in the skillet or pan on all sides. This does not happen in an air fryer, because the air is not strong enough to separate the ingredients. To avoid undercooked food, you will need to open the machine at least once to shake the ingredients in the basket while cooking. Most people remove the basket halfway through the cooking to shake the ingredients. For example, if you were to set a timer for twenty minutes, you would need to pause the fryer after ten minutes and mix the ingredients before you restart the fryer again.

Keep it Light

One mistake most people make when using the air fryer is that they overload it. When you deep-fry food, you know the quantity of food that needs to be cooked in the oil, but when you use an air fryer, you may not leave enough space for the ingredients to cook properly. If you ever hear of people complaining about how their air fryer doesn't make their food crispy, then they are probably making this mistake. Meat needs to be cooked in a single layer, just like it does in a traditional oven. Read the manual carefully to ensure you do not overload the basket.

Preheat the Air Fryer

Warm up your air fryer to the cooking temperature for at least three minutes before adding the ingredients.

Cut Your Food to Uniform Sizes for the Best Results

Smaller pieces will be crispier, and consistent sizing will help the food to cook evenly.

Use Cooking Spray

Although the air fryer manual says you don't need to add oil, you may need to use a teaspoon of oil to ensure your food has the best taste. If you do not want to use oil, you can use cooking spray, otherwise, your food may stick to the air fryer basket.

Start with Room Temperature

When you cook using fresh ingredients, do not start cooking them immediately after you take them out of the fridge. Let the ingredients warm to room temperature before placing them in the fryer. This will reduce the cooking time and will also give you crispier results.

Do More with It

Although this appliance is called an air "fryer", it does a lot more than just fry food. You can make anything from noodles to a pizza in an air fryer. An air fryer has more in common with a fan-forced oven rather than a deep fryer. You can roast, bake, and grill in an air fryer. In other words, experiment!

Take Good Care

To take good care of your air fryer, you don't have to clean it constantly, but like every other electronic appliance, it does need a certain level of care. If you use your air fryer regularly, you will need to clean it every five to ten days to prevent unwanted smells. Use a dishwasher to clean the removable parts of the fryer or soak them in soapy water before cleaning them gently with a sponge.

Air fryers are very popular right now as a great way to cook crispy, delicious, and healthy food. It saves time and is a perfect addition to busy households. If you love fried food this home cooking trend is one to get behind! This book provides you with 105 easy and tasty air fryer recipes, some taking as little as a few minutes to prepare.

CHAPTER TWO

Breakfast

Quick Breakfast Frittata

Yield: 10 servings

Ingredients:

4 cherry tomatoes, halved
1 cup sausage, crumbled
4 large eggs
1 tablespoon olive oil
4 tablespoons fresh parsley, chopped
½ cup parmesan cheese, grated
Salt and pepper to taste

Directions:

1. Preheat the air fryer to 390 degrees F.
2. Insert a small pan and put the cherry tomatoes and crumbled sausage in the pan.
3. Cook for 6–7 minutes.
4. In a bowl, whisk together the eggs, parsley, cheese, salt, and pepper.
5. Pour the egg mixture over the tomatoes and sausage.
6. Bake in the air fryer for 5–6 more minutes.

Cheese Omelet

Yield: 1 serving

Ingredients:

2 large eggs

1 onion, diced

⅛ teaspoon hot sauce

¼ cup cheddar cheese, grated

Salt and pepper to taste

Directions:

1. Preheat the air fryer to 360 degrees F.
2. In a bowl, whisk the eggs until fluffy and stir in the hot sauce, salt, and pepper.
3. Place a small pan inside the air fryer and spray with a non-stick cooking spray.
4. Put the onions in the pan and cook for 10 minutes.
5. Pour the whisked eggs over the onions and top with the cheddar cheese.
6. Cook the omelet for another 5 minutes.

Easy Egg Potato Hash

Yield: 2 servings

Ingredients:

3 eggs

¼ teaspoon garlic powder

¼ teaspoon paprika

Pinch of nutmeg

Salt and pepper to taste

1 cup flour

1 large potato, peeled and grated

Directions:

1. Set your air fryer to 390 degrees F.
2. In a bowl, beat the eggs along with the spices.
3. Season with some salt and pepper to taste and whisk in the flour.
4. Fold in the shredded potato and then shape the mixture into patties.
5. Spray the bottom of the air fryer with some cooking spray, and arrange the patties inside.
6. Bake for 15 minutes.
7. Serve and enjoy!

Breakfast Burrito

Yield: 2 servings

Ingredients:

2 large eggs

4 thin slices turkey or chicken

4 tablespoons bell pepper, diced

6 thin avocado slices

3 tablespoons grated mozzarella

2 tortillas

3 tablespoons salsa

Salt and pepper to taste

Directions:

1. Preheat air fryer to 360 degrees F.
2. Whisk the eggs in a bowl and add the salt and pepper.
3. Place a small pan inside the basket of the air fryer. Spray the pan with a non-stick cooking spray.
4. Pour the eggs into the pan and cook for 5 minutes.
5. Carefully remove the pan from the air fryer.
6. Fill the tortillas with equal amounts of egg, turkey or chicken, bell pepper, avocado, grated cheese, and salsa. Be careful not to overstuff the tortillas.
7. Roll and firmly wrap the tortillas.
8. Place the tortillas on a tray in the air fryer.
9. Decrease the temperature to 350 degrees F and cook for 3 minutes.
10. Serve hot, with salsa on the side.

Blueberry Muffins

Yield: 5–6 servings

Ingredients:

1 cup blueberries
1½ cups flour
⅓ cup white sugar
2 teaspoons baking powder
½ teaspoon salt
1 large egg
1 cup plain yogurt
⅓ cup canola oil
2 teaspoons vanilla
2 tablespoons brown sugar

Directions:

1. Wash and place blueberries in a bowl and coat thoroughly with one tablespoon of the flour.
2. In another bowl, mix remaining flour, sugar, baking powder, and salt. Stir well to combine.
3. In a third bowl, whisk the egg, yogurt, and oil. Stir in vanilla.
4. Add the egg mixture to dry ingredients and stir well.
5. Fold the blueberries into batter.
6. Place 5–6 muffin cups inside air fryer basket.
7. Pour batter equally among muffin cups.
8. Sprinkle dash of brown sugar on top of each muffin.
9. Heat the air fryer to 360 degrees F and cook for 10 minutes.
10. Check for doneness by sticking a toothpick in the center of a muffin. Toothpick should come out clean.
11. If necessary, cook another 2 minutes.

Oreo Cakes

Yield: 4 servings

Ingredients:

10 Oreo biscuits

1 cup milk

½ teaspoon baking soda

1 teaspoon baking powder

1 tablespoon chopped nuts

Directions:

1. Preheat air fryer to 390 degrees F.
2. Add biscuits to a grinder and grind into a semi-fine powder.
3. Add milk to a bowl along with baking soda and baking powder, and mix until well combined.
4. Add in nuts and biscuit powder, and mix until well combined.
5. Add it to a baking tray and place in the fryer.
6. Bake for 3 minutes at 390 degrees F.
7. Serve warm.

Cheddar Bacon Balls

Yield: 6 servings

Ingredients:

1 pound block of cheddar cheese
12 strips of bacon
2 eggs
1 cup flour
2 tablespoons olive oil
½ cup breadcrumbs
1 teaspoon salt
1 teaspoon pepper
1 tablespoon dried parsley

Directions:

1. Divide the block of cheese into 6 squares.
2. Wrap two pieces of bacon around each chunk of cheese. Make sure all the cheese is covered and any excess bacon fat is cut off the block.
3. Place these bacon and cheese chunks in the freezer for 3–5 minutes.
4. Preheat your air fryer to 390 degrees F.
5. Combine the breadcrumbs with the salt, pepper, and parsley. Stir in the oil.
6. Place the eggs in a separate bowl and whisk lightly with a fork.
7. Dip the cheddar blocks into the flour and coat, then the eggs, and then the breadcrumbs.
8. Place these into the cooking basket and cook for 8 minutes. They will come out golden brown.

Sausage Biscuits

Yield: 4 servings

Ingredients:

8 frozen breakfast sausage patties

8 refrigerated biscuits

2 slices of provolone or American cheese

Ketchup or syrup for serving

Directions:

1. Preheat your air fryer to 375 degrees F.

2. Cut each slice of cheese into fourths so you have 8 small pieces.

3. Separate the biscuit dough. Layer sausage patties and cheese on 4 of the biscuits so that there are 2 patties and 2 cheese pieces on 4 of the biscuit rounds.

3. Place the remaining 4 biscuit rounds on top.

4. Cook for 4 minutes in the air fryer.

5. Remove to cool and serve with ketchup or syrup.

French Toast Triangles

Yield: 2 servings

Ingredients:

4 pieces of your favorite bread

2 eggs, beaten

2 tablespoons butter

1 teaspoon salt

2 teaspoons cinnamon

1 teaspoon nutmeg

Powdered sugar and syrup for serving

Directions:

1. Preheat your air fryer to 350 degrees F.
2. Beat the eggs in a bowl and add salt, cinnamon, and nutmeg.
3. Butter each side of the bread slices, and cut them diagonally so you have four wedges for each slice. Soak each wedge in the egg mixture and arrange in the Air Fryer basket (you will need to cook more than one batch).
4. Cook in the air fryer for 3 minutes.
5. Flip the toast wedges over to the other side and cook for another 3 minutes.
6. Dust with powdered sugar or drizzle with syrup.

Cheese and Herb Frittata

Yield: 2 servings

Ingredients:

4 eggs

1 teaspoon butter, melted

¼ cup shredded cheddar cheese

¼ cup shredded gruyere cheese

1 tablespoon fresh rosemary, chopped

1 tablespoon fresh parsley, chopped

1 tablespoon fresh sage, chopped

1 tablespoon fresh basil, chopped

2 tablespoons milk

Directions:

1. Preheat the air fryer to 350 degrees F.

2. Beat the eggs with the milk and add the cheese, butter, and herbs.

3. Pour the mixture directly into the air fryer pan and leave it to cook for 15 minutes.

Soufflé

Yield: 2 servings

Ingredients:

2 eggs

2 tablespoons cream

1 tablespoon red pepper flakes

1 tablespoon fresh parsley

Directions:

1. Preheat the air fryer to 400 degrees F.
2. In a bowl, combine eggs with cream, red pepper flakes, and parsley. Pour into two soufflé cups and set in the air fryer.
3. Cook for 5 minutes if you want soft eggs and 8 minutes if you prefer hard eggs.

Egg Cups with Bacon

Yield: 4 servings

Ingredients:

1 tablespoon butter

6 ounces bacon

¼ teaspoon salt

½ teaspoon paprika

4 eggs

½ teaspoon dried dill

Directions:

1. Preheat the air fryer to 350 degrees F.
2. Whisk the eggs in a bowl and add the salt, paprika, and dried dill.
3. Coat 4 ramekins with butter. Slice the bacon and place inside the ramekins.
4. Transfer the egg mixture to the 4 ramekins.
5. Place the ramekins in the cooking basket and cook for 15 minutes.
6. Serve warm.

Cheese and Egg

Yield: 4 servings

Ingredients:

1 egg yolk

4 ounces fresh feta cheese

2 tablespoons cilantro leaves, chopped

1 shallot, finely chopped

2 sheets filo pastry (store bought or homemade)

2 tablespoons olive oil

Salt and pepper to taste

Directions:

1. Preheat air fryer to 390 degrees F.
2. Add egg yolk to a bowl and beat until frothy.
3. Add in feta cheese and shallots, and mix until well combined.
4. Add in cilantro, pepper, and salt and beat further.
5. Lay filo pastry on a plate and cut it into squares.
6. Fill each square with the filling and cover with another square. Use a little water to apply at the edges and press down gently to seal the filling in.
7. Use a brush to apply olive oil over the dumplings. Carefully place them in the basket.

Reduce temperature to 360 degrees F. Cook for 5 to 10 minutes.

8. Serve hot.

CHAPTER THREE

Lunch

Vegetable Salad with Vinaigrette

Yield: 6 servings

Ingredients:

1 white cauliflower, chopped into florets
1 purple cauliflower, chopped into florets
3 beets, peeled and chopped into bite-size pieces
1 teaspoon olive oil
4 cups endives, chopped
1 cup arugula, chopped
6 radishes, sliced
½ cup mint, chopped

For the Vinaigrette:

½ cup parsley
½ cup cilantro
¼ cup chives
1 shallot, minced
1 garlic clove, minced
3 tablespoons lemon juice
⅓ cup red wine vinegar
½ cup olive oil
Salt and pepper to taste

Directions:

1. Preheat the air fryer to 360 degrees F.
2. Place the cauliflower in a bowl, and coat with a little olive oil.
3. In another bowl, add the beets, and coat with a little olive oil.

4. Add the cauliflower to the basket of the air fryer. Cook for 8 minutes and transfer to a plate.

5. Place the beets in the fry basket and cook for 12 minutes. Transfer to a plate.

6. For the vinaigrette, put the parsley, cilantro, chives, shallot, garlic, lemon juice, and vinegar in a blender. Puree ingredients while slowly adding the olive oil.

7. Toss the cauliflower and beets in a large bowl.

8. Add the endive and arugula. Pour the vinaigrette over the salad.

9. Garnish the salad with the radishes and mint.

Avocado Egg Boats

Yield: 2 servings

Ingredients:

1 avocado, sliced in half

2 small eggs

1 tablespoon fresh parsley, chopped

Salt and pepper to taste

Directions:

1. Preheat the air fryer to 390 degrees F.
2. Remove the pit from the avocado. Crack an egg into each half of the avocado.
3. Place in the air fryer basket and cook for 8 minutes.
4. Sprinkle with parsley, salt, and pepper.
5. Serve and enjoy!

Fried Rice Casserole

Yield: 4 servings

Ingredients:

2 cups cooked rice

1 tablespoon butter

1 medium red onion, chopped

4 garlic cloves, chopped

3 tablespoons broccoli florets

2 tablespoons carrot cubes

2 sausages, chopped

3 tablespoons cheddar cheese, shredded

2 tablespoons mozzarella cheese, shredded

Directions:

1. Preheat air fryer to 390 degrees F.
2. Add butter and onions to a pan and sauté over medium-high heat.
3. Add garlic, carrots, broccoli, and sausage and cook until soft. Transfer to a baking dish and top with cooked rice.
4. Sprinkle cheeses on top and place in air fryer.
5. Bake for 10 to 15 minutes and serve hot.

Pepperoni Pizza

Yield: 2 servings

Ingredients:

½ pound fresh pizza dough

½ cup prepared pizza sauce

¼ cup pepperoni slices or chunks

¼ cup mushrooms, sliced

¼ cup shredded mozzarella cheese

1 teaspoon dried oregano

8 muffin tins

Directions:

1. Preheat air fryer to 400 degrees F.

2. Press pizza dough into the muffin tins.

3. In a bowl, mix the pizza sauce, pepperoni, mushrooms, cheese, and oregano. Spoon into the muffin tins.

4. Cook in air fryer for 10 minutes.

Cheesy Eggplant Sandwich

Yield: 2 servings

Ingredients:

½ cup breadcrumbs
2 tablespoons grated parmesan cheese
½ teaspoon Italian seasoning
¼ teaspoon onion powder
¼ teaspoon garlic powder
Salt and pepper to taste
2 tablespoons milk
½ cup mayo
1 medium eggplant, sliced
¼ cup tomato sauce
4 slices Italian bread
½ cups shredded mozzarella cheese

Directions:

1. Preheat your air fryer to 400 degrees F.
2. In a shallow dish, combine the breadcrumbs, parmesan, and the spices and seasonings.
3. In another bowl, whisk together the mayo and milk.
4. Dip the eggplant slices in the milk/mayo mixture and then coat with the breadcrumbs.
5. Arrange them inside the air fryer and spray with some cooking spray.
6. Cook for 15 minutes, turning them over once.
7. Divide the eggplants between 2 bread slices.
8. Top with tomato sauce and mozzarella.
9. Place the other bread slices on top.
10. Serve and enjoy!

Fried Tofu

Yield: 4 servings

Ingredients:

1 block of tofu, chopped into cubes

2 tablespoons cornstarch

¼ cup rice flour

¼ cup Parmesan cheese, grated

Salt and pepper to taste

2 tablespoons olive oil

Directions:

1. Preheat air fryer to 390 degrees F.
2. Add cornstarch, rice flour, salt, pepper, and oil to a bowl and mix until well combined.
3. Add tofu cubes and coat them thoroughly.
4. Add to the basket and fry for 15 to 20 minutes or until crispy.
5. Serve hot, with a sauce of your choice.

Fried Ravioli with Marinara

Yield: 3 servings

Ingredients:

1 package (16 ounces) fresh ravioli

2 eggs

1 cup seasoned Italian bread crumbs

¼ cup grated parmesan cheese

1 cup prepared marinara sauce

Cooking spray

Directions:

1. Preheat the air fryer to 400 degrees F.
2. Whisk the eggs in a bowl and place the bread crumbs in a separate bowl.
3. Dip the raviolis in the egg mixture and then in the bread crumbs, coating them and giving them a shake.
4. Lay the raviolis out on a baking sheet or plate. Spray lightly with cooking spray.
5. Place the raviolis into the fryer and cook for 5 minutes on each side.
6. Sprinkle with parmesan cheese and dip into the marinara sauce. This goes well with crusty bread or a big salad.

Baked Eggs and Tomatoes

Yield: 2 servings

Ingredients:

1 tomato, sliced

2 eggs

2 tablespoons whole milk or cream

3 tablespoons cheddar cheese, grated

Salt and pepper to taste

Optional: 1 teaspoon of your favorite herbs

Directions:

1. Heat the air fryer to 360 degrees F.
2. Divide the sliced tomato between 2 ramekins.
3. Add the salt and pepper, and any herbs of your choice.
4. In a bowl, whisk the eggs and milk together.
5. Transfer the egg mixture to the 2 ramekins. Top with the grated cheese.
6. Place the ramekins in the basket of the air fryer. Cook for 10 minutes.
7. Serve with hot sauce, sour cream, or salsa.

Roasted Chick Peas

Yield: 4 servings
Ingredients:
2 cans chick peas
1 tablespoon olive oil
1 tablespoon garlic powder
1 tablespoon dried rosemary
1 tablespoon dried parsley
1 tablespoon dried oregano
Salt and pepper to taste

Directions:

1. Preheat the air fryer to 390 degrees F.
2. Drain and rinse the chick peas.
3. In a bowl, combine the chick peas with the olive oil and seasonings. Mix together until combined and coated.
4. Cook in the air fryer basket for about 15 minutes in two separate batches. You may hear a popping noise while they cook. This is normal, but it may be a good idea to give them a stir halfway through the cooking process.

Thyme and Basil Bruschetta

Yield: 4 servings

Ingredients:

4 Roma tomatoes
1 tablespoon olive oil
1 clove garlic, minced
1 teaspoon dried thyme
1 teaspoon dried basil
Salt and pepper
Crostini or crackers

Directions:

1. Preheat the air fryer to 390 degrees F.
2. Slice the tomatoes in half and scoop out all the seeds and pulp.
3. In a bowl, toss the tomatoes with the olive oil, garlic, and herbs.
4. Place the tomatoes into the air fryer, with the open sides facing up. Cook for about 15 minutes.
5. Let the tomatoes cool, and serve on top of the crostini or crackers.

Cheddar Croquettes with Bacon

Yield: 6 servings

Ingredients:

1 pound sharp cheddar cheese

½ pound bacon

1 tablespoons olive oil

½ cup panko breadcrumbs

1 cup flour

2 eggs, beaten

Directions:

1. Slice cheddar cheese into 1-inch pieces.
2. Wrap a bacon slice around each piece. Place in freezer for 10 minutes.
3. Preheat the air fryer to 370 degrees F.
4. Combine the olive oil and breadcrumbs.
5. In separate dishes place the flour, the breadcrumbs, and the eggs.
6. Coat the cheese with the flour, then dip in the eggs, and press into the breadcrumbs.
7. Transfer the croquettes to the cooking basket and cook for approximately 8 minutes, or until golden brown.

Cheesy Balls

Yield: 4 servings

Ingredients:

2 potatoes

½ teaspoon red chili powder

½ teaspoon turmeric powder

½ teaspoon breadcrumbs

½ teaspoon pepper

Cheese cubes

Salt to taste

Directions:

1. Preheat air fryer to 360 degrees F.
2. Add potatoes to boiling water and cook until tender, about 15 to 20 minutes.
3. Meanwhile, add breadcrumbs, chili powder, turmeric powder, pepper, and salt to a bowl and mix until well combined.
4. Add potatoes to the mix and mash them in. Make roundlets out of the mix and press it flat. Place a cheese cube at the center and close the roundlet.
5. Apply vegetable oil on the surface of the roundlets. Place them in the air fryer.
6. Fry for 5 minutes at 360 degrees F.
7. Serve hot, with a sauce of your choice.

Spicy Shrimp over Rice

Yield: 4 servings
Ingredients:
2 cups cooked rice
1 pound medium shrimp
½ teaspoon cayenne pepper
½ teaspoon paprika
½ teaspoon red pepper flakes
1 teaspoon Old Bay seasoning
2 tablespoons olive oil
Salt to taste.

Directions:

1. Prepare the rice and set aside until it's ready to be topped with shrimp.
2. Preheat air fryer to 390 degrees F.
3. Combine the shrimp with the oil and all the seasonings until coated.
4. Cook the shrimp in the basket for 6 minutes.
5. Serve on the rice.

CHAPTER FOUR

Snacks and Appetizers

Air Fried French Fries

Yield: 4 servings

Ingredients:

4 russet potatoes
2 tablespoons olive oil
1 tablespoon salt
2 tablespoons ketchup
2 tablespoons mustard
2 tablespoons ranch dressing
2 tablespoons barbeque sauce

Directions:

1. Scrub the potatoes and cut them into strips, lengthwise.
2. Soak them in a bowl of cool water for 30 minutes.
3. Preheat the air fryer to 400 degrees F.
4. Once potatoes are dry, toss them with olive oil and salt.
5. Cook them in the fryer basket for 15 minutes.
6. Be sure to shake the basket after 7 minutes to ensure the fries don't stick to one another. Remove them from the fryer and enjoy them with the selection of dipping sauces.
7. Add additional salt and pepper if necessary.

Mozzarella Sticks

Yield: 2 servings

Ingredients:

4 ounces mozzarella cheese

½ cup breadcrumbs

1 small egg

Pinch of salt

½ teaspoon garlic powder

Directions:

1. Beat the egg with the salt and garlic powder.
2. Cut the mozzarella into sticks and dip them in the egg mixture.
3. In a shallow dish, press the sticks into the breadcrumbs.
4. Arrange on a lined baking sheet and place in the freezer for at least 20 minutes.
5. Meanwhile, preheat your air fryer to 370 degrees F.
6. Grease the bottom of the air fryer with some cooking spray and arrange the mozzarella sticks inside.
7. Fry for 5 minutes. Make sure to turn them over at least once to ensure an even golden color.

Spring Rolls

Yield: 4 servings

Ingredients:

For the Filling:

4 ounces cooked chicken breast, pulled
1 celery stalk, thinly sliced
1 medium carrot, thinly sliced
½ cup mushrooms, thinly sliced
½ teaspoon ginger, minced
1 teaspoon brown sugar
1 teaspoon chicken stock powder
Salt and pepper to taste

For the Wrappers:

1 egg, beaten
1 teaspoon cornstarch
8 spring roll wrappers
½ teaspoon vegetable oil

Directions:

1. Preheat air fryer to 390 degrees F.
2. Add chicken, celery, carrot, mushrooms, ginger, sugar, and chicken stock to a bowl and mix until well combined.
3. Add in salt and pepper to taste.
4. Place a wrapper on a plate and add 1 tbsp. of the filling.
5. In a bowl, mix the cornstarch and egg together. Use the egg mixture to line the sides of the wrapper. Roll into a spring roll.
6. Apply oil to top of each roll and place them in the basket.
7. Fry for 3 to 4 minutes at 360 F or until golden on the outside.
8. Serve with a sauce of your choice.

Old Fashioned Onion Rings

Yield: 4 servings

Ingredients:

1 cup flour

1½ teaspoons baking powder

1 teaspoon salt

1 onion, sliced

¾ cup milk

1 egg, beaten

¾ cup panko breadcrumbs

Directions:

1. Preheat the air fryer to 360 degrees F.
2. Mix together the flour, baking powder, and salt.
3. Coat each onion slice with the flour mixture.
4. Whisk together the milk and egg.
5. Dip each onion ring in the egg mixture.
6. In a shallow dish, press the onion rings into the breadcrumbs.
7. Transfer the battered onion rings to the air fryer; cook for approximately 10 minutes, or until brown.

Butter Cookies

Yield: 8 servings

Ingredients:

½ cup gram flour

1 cup semolina

1 cup sugar

1 teaspoon vanilla extract

1 tablespoon butter, melted

Directions:

1. Add flour, semolina, and sugar to a bowl and mix until well combined.
2. Mix butter and vanilla in a bowl and add to flour.
3. Preheat air fryer to 390 degrees F.
4. Knead mix into dough and make small rounds from it.
5. Add to basket and bake for 10 minutes or until biscuits turn crispy.
6. Serve once cooled.
7. These biscuits will keep well for a week or two in an air-tight container.

Eggplant Strips

Yield: 4 servings

Ingredients:

1 large eggplant
2 tablespoons olive oil
½ cup bread crumbs
¼ cup grated parmesan cheese
1 tablespoon garlic salt
1 tablespoon dried parsley
1 tablespoon dried oregano
Salt and pepper to taste
¼ cup prepared spicy mayo

Directions:

1. Preheat air fryer to 400 degrees F.
2. Wash the eggplant and pat dry. Cut it in half lengthwise and then slice into strips. Cut the long strips in half. Sprinkle with salt and pepper and drizzle with olive oil. Toss to ensure all the strips are coated.
3. In a bowl, combine the bread crumbs, cheese, and spices.
4. Add the eggplant strips to the mixture, coating.
5. Cook in the fryer for 5 minutes, and give the basket a shake.
6. Cook for another 3 minutes.
7. Serve with spicy mayo or your favorite dipping sauce.

Jalapeno Poppers

Yield: 3 servings

Ingredients:

6 jalapeno peppers

3–4 ounces cheddar cheese

3 spring roll wrappers

2 eggs, beaten

Ranch or mayo dipping sauce

Cooking spray

Directions:

1. Preheat air fryer to 350 degrees F.
2. Cut the stem and end from the peppers and slice them lengthwise, scooping out the seeds.
3. Divide the cheese into strips.
4. Cut each spring roll wrapper in half and brush with the beaten egg liquid. Place half a jalapeno in each wrapper and put a strip of cheese inside the pepper. Top with the other half of the jalapeno pepper. Holding the pepper together, roll it in the wrapper. Fold the edges in and make sure there are no loose pieces.
5. Brush any loose pieces with egg to keep them glued together. Spray them lightly with cooking spray and place in the fryer.
6. Cook for 10–12 minutes and serve hot, with your favorite dipping sauce.

Grilled Cheese

Yield: 4 servings

Ingredients:

4 ounces feta cheese

1 egg yolk

4 sheets frozen phyllo dough, defrosted

1 green onion, chopped finely

2 tablespoons fresh parsley, chopped

2 tablespoons fresh basil, chopped

2 tablespoons olive oil

Salt and pepper to taste

Directions:

1. Preheat the air fryer to 390 degrees F.
2. Cut the phyllo dough into three strips. Brush each one with olive oil.
3. In a bowl, beat the egg with the cheese, onion, parsley, basil, salt, and pepper.
4. Spoon a teaspoon or so of the mixture onto a strip of dough and fold it over to create a triangle.
5. Place the triangles in the basket and cook for 3 minutes.

Easy Crab Sticks

Yield: 4 servings
Ingredients:
1 pack crab sticks of your choice
2 tablespoons olive oil
Salt and pepper to taste

Directions:
1. Preheat air fryer to 320 degrees F.
2. Place crab sticks on a plate and sprinkle with salt and pepper.
3. Apply oil on top of crab sticks and add to the air fryer.
4. Fry for 10 minutes or until crispy and serve.

Donut Holes

Yield: 6 servings

Ingredients:

2 tablespoons butter, softened plus an extra tablespoon that's melted

½ cup sugar

2¼ cups flour

1½ teaspoons baking powder

1 teaspoon salt

2 large egg yolks

½ cup plain yogurt

2 tablespoons cinnamon

2 tablespoons powdered sugar

Directions:

1. Preheat the fryer to 350 degrees F.
2. In one bowl, combine the butter and sugar until it crumbles. Add the egg yolks and mix until smooth.
3. In a separate bowl, sift the flour, baking powder, and salt together.
4. Add the yogurt to the sugar mixture and combine. Then, add that to the flour mixture by the spoonful and mix together.
5. Roll into small round balls. Brush with melted butter.
6. Cook in the fryer for 6 minutes. Remove them and immediately roll in either the powdered sugar or the cinnamon.

Sweet Potato Fries

Yield: 6 servings

Ingredients:

1 pound sweet potatoes

1 tablespoon vegetable oil

Directions:

1. Preheat air fryer to 340 degrees F.
2. Peel and cut potatoes into fries and place in a bowl.
3. Toss fries with the oil. It's okay to use your hands.
4. Add fries to basket and cook for approximately 15 min.
5. Shake basket to distribute the fries in the basket. Cook at 360 degrees F for 5 more minutes.
6. Shake basket and cook another 5 minutes.

Fried Dough with Amaretto Sauce

Yield: 20 servings

Ingredients:

1 pound bread or pizza dough

½ cup melted, unsalted butter

½ cup sugar

1 cup heavy cream

12 ounces semi-sweet chocolate chips

2 tablespoons amaretto liqueur

Directions:

1. Roll out dough and form a log.
2. Cut the log into 20 pieces.
3. Halve each piece and twist the two halves together a few times to create a cork screw effect.
4. Place the dough slices on a baking sheet, brush with the melted butter, and top with the sugar.
5. Preheat the air fryer to 350 degrees F and brush a little melted butter on bottom of the basket.
6. In batches, air fry the dough for 5 minutes.
7. Turn the pieces over, brush the other sides with more butter and air fry another 3 minutes.
8. For the amaretto sauce, place the chocolate chips in a bowl.
9. Simmer the heavy cream in a pan until heated thoroughly. Pour the heavy cream over the chocolate chips and whisk until smooth. Add the amaretto liqueur.
10. Coat the air fried dough pieces with more sugar and serve with the sauce.

CHAPTER FIVE

Poultry

Buffalo Style Chicken Wings

Yield: 5 servings

Ingredients:

3 cups water
¼ cup salt
¼ cup brown sugar
1 teaspoon cayenne powder
10 chicken wings
1 cup rice flour
4 tablespoons unsalted butter, melted
4 tablespoons hot sauce
1 teaspoon apple cider vinegar
1 teaspoon soy sauce
1 teaspoon ketchup
Salt to taste

Directions:

1. Preheat air fryer to 390 degrees F.
2. Add water to a bowl along with salt and sugar and prepare a brine.
3. Add chicken pieces to it and allow it to sit for 2 to 12 hours in the fridge.
4. Add cayenne, butter, flour, hot sauce, vinegar, soy sauce, and ketchup and mix until well combined.
5. Allow it to soak for 2 to 3 hours.
6. Pat dry before placing in fryer. Cook for 15 minutes at 390 degrees F.
7. Give it a shake at the half-way mark.

8. Check to see if they have crisped. If not, fry for a further 10 minutes.

9. Serve hot.

Fried Chicken Sandwich

Yield: 2 servings

Ingredients:

2 chicken breasts, boneless and skinless

2 large eggs

½ cup whole milk

1 cup flour

2 tablespoons sugar

½ teaspoon garlic powder

2 tablespoons olive oil

2 hamburger buns

Salt and pepper to taste

Directions:

1. Heat the air fry to 350 degrees F.
2. Place the chicken breasts in a plastic bag and use a mallet to pound the meat to a ½-inch thickness.
3. Cut the chicken into several large pieces.
4. Whisk the eggs and milk in a bowl.
5. In another bowl, stir the flour with the sugar, garlic powder, salt, and pepper.
6. Dip the chicken pieces in the egg mixture, then coat them with the flour mixture.
7. Spray the bottom of the air fryer with a non-stick cooking spray. Cook chicken for 5 minutes.
8. Flip the chicken and cook another 6 minutes.
9. Increase the heat to 390 degrees F and cook 2 more minutes.
10. Toast the hamburger buns and assemble the sandwiches.
11. If desired, add mayonnaise and pickles.

Honey Lemon Chicken

Yield: 6 servings

Ingredients:

For the Chicken:

1 whole chicken (4 pounds)
2 tablespoons olive oil
2 red onions, peeled and chopped
1 green zucchini, chopped
1 red bell pepper, chopped
2 apricots
2 cloves garlic, minced
Fresh thyme, chopped
Salt and pepper to taste

For the Marinade:

1 cup honey
1 large lemon, juiced
2 tablespoons olive oil
Salt and pepper to taste

Directions:

1. Mix honey, lemon juice, olive oil, salt, and pepper in a bowl and mix until well combined.
2. Brush mixture over chicken, and marinate in fridge for 12 to 24 hours.
3. Preheat air fryer to 390 degrees F.
4. Heat olive oil in a pan over medium-high heat. Add onions and garlic and sauté until brown.
5. Add apricots, bell pepper, thyme, salt, and pepper and mix until well combined.
6. Open the cavity of the chicken and fill with filling.
7. Place chicken in a baking dish and put in the air fryer. Fry for 30 minutes.

8. Flip chicken over, and fry for another 20 to 30 minutes, or until the chicken turns crispy.

9. Serve hot.

Crispy Chicken Wings

Yield: 6 servings

Ingredients:

3 pounds chicken wings
2 tablespoons olive oil
2 tablespoons dark soy sauce
6 garlic cloves, finely chopped
4 jalapeno peppers, finely chopped
1 tablespoon allspice powder
1 teaspoon cinnamon powder
1 teaspoon cayenne pepper powder
1 teaspoon white pepper powder
1 teaspoon salt
2 tablespoons brown sugar
1 tablespoon fresh thyme, finely chopped
1 tablespoon fresh ginger, grated
4 scallions, finely chopped
5 tablespoons lime juice
½ cup red wine vinegar

Directions:

1. Preheat air fryer to 390 degrees F.
2. In a large bowl, add chicken wings and all the other ingredients except for olive oil. Mix until well combined.
3. Marinate for 24 hours in fridge.
4. Use paper towel to pat chicken wings dry. Brush olive oil onto the wings.
5. Add wings to basket and set time to 15 minutes.
6. Shake basket at the 7-and-a-half-minute mark to distribute the wings in the basket.
7. Check at the 15-minute mark if the wings are crispy enough. If not, fry for 4 more minutes.
8. Serve hot.

Turkey Breast with Savory Glaze

Yield: 4–6 servings

Ingredients:

4–5 pounds turkey breast

2 teaspoons olive oil

1 teaspoon thyme

½ teaspoon sage

Salt and pepper to taste

¼ cup maple syrup

2 tablespoons Dijon mustard

1 tablespoon softened butter

Directions:

1. Preheat the air fryer to 350 degrees F.
2. Coat the entire turkey breast with the olive oil.
3. Combine the spices and coat the turkey breast with the mix.
4. Place the turkey breast into the air fryer. Cook for 25 minutes.
5. Turn the turkey breast to its side and cook for 12 minutes.
6. Turn to the other side and cook for another 12 minutes.
7. For the glaze, combine the syrup, mustard, and butter.
8. Reset the turkey breast to its original position and brush on the glaze.
9. Cook for another 5 minutes.
10. Let turkey rest 10 minutes before serving.

Easy Buffalo Ranch Chicken Wings

Yield: 2 servings

Ingredients:

1 pound chicken wings, drums, and flats

¼ cup wing sauce

¼ cup ranch dressing

Directions:

1. Preheat your air fryer to 375 degrees F.
2. Put the wings in the fryer basket and cook for 15 minutes.
3. Take the basket out and shake or turn the wings to ensure even heating. Cook for another 10 minutes.
4. Pour into a bowl and cover with wing sauce and ranch.

Buttermilk Chicken

Yield: 4–6 servings

Ingredients:

2 pounds chicken thighs

Salt and pepper to taste

1 tablespoon garlic powder

1 tablespoon paprika

2 cups buttermilk

2 cups flour

Directions:

1. Wash chicken thighs thoroughly and pat dry.
2. In a bowl, mix together pepper, salt, garlic powder, and paprika.
3. Rub chicken pieces with the mixture and refrigerate overnight.
4. Preheat air fryer to 360 degrees F.
5. Dip chicken in the buttermilk, then coat with the flour.
6. Transfer chicken to fryer basket and set in one layer.
7. Cook for 10 minutes, turn chicken, and cook for another 10 minutes.

Chicken Satay

Yield: 4 servings

Ingredients:

12 ounces boneless, skinless, chicken tenders
2 tablespoons soy sauce
½ cup orange juice
1 tablespoon sesame oil
4 garlic cloves, chopped
2 scallions, chopped
1 tablespoon fresh ginger, grated
2 teaspoons sesame seeds, toasted
1 pinch black pepper
Salt to taste

Directions:

1. Preheat air fryer to 390 degrees F.
2. Add chicken to a bowl along with soy sauce, orange juice, sesame oil, garlic, scallions, ginger, sesame seeds, pepper, and salt. Mix and marinate for 2 to 5 hours in the fridge.
3. Use skewers to pierce through chicken pieces.
4. Place in basket and fry for 5 to 7 minutes or until crisp.
5. Serve with sauce of your choice.

Chicken Cordon Bleu

Yield: 4 servings

Ingredients:

2 chicken breasts
1 tablespoon tarragon
Salt and pepper to taste
2 tablespoons cream cheese
1 teaspoon parsley
1 tablespoon garlic powder
2 slices Swiss cheese
2 slices cooked ham
1 large egg, beaten
¼ cup breadcrumbs

Directions:

1. Preheat the air fryer to 360 degrees F.
2. Season chicken with the tarragon, salt, and pepper.
3. Use a sharp knife to cut a slit in the middle of each breast.
4. Mix the cream cheese, parsley, and garlic powder, and spoon into the opening in each breast.
5. Cut the Swiss cheese slice and ham slices in two, and add 1 slice each to breasts.
6. Press to seal the opening and keep the stuffing inside.
7. With the beaten egg on one plate and the breadcrumbs in another, dip each breast into the beaten egg and then press into the breadcrumbs.
8. Transfer the chicken breasts to the air fryer.
9. Cook at 360 degrees F for 15 minutes.
10. Flip the chicken breasts over and cook for another 15 minutes.

Chicken Tandoori

Yield: 4 servings

Ingredients:

4 chicken thighs

Salt and pepper to taste

½ teaspoon chili paste

½ teaspoon garlic paste

¼ teaspoon garam masala powder

¼ teaspoon coriander

¼ teaspoon cumin

1 teaspoon lime juice

2 tablespoon Greek yogurt

1 teaspoon olive oil

Directions:

1. Use a sharp knife to score the chicken thighs in several places.
2. Combine all other ingredients except for the olive oil in a bowl.
3. Thoroughly coat the chicken with the spice mix and refrigerate for a few hours.
4. Preheat the air fryer to 380 degrees F.
5. Add the chicken thighs and cook for 10 minutes.
6. Remove the chicken from the basket and brush with the olive oil.
7. Return chicken to the air fryer and cook for 5 more minutes.
8. Serve with rice.

Jerk Chicken Drumsticks

Yield: 4 servings

Ingredients:

1 pound chicken drumsticks
2 tablespoons olive oil
2 tablespoons freshly squeezed lime juice
4 green onions, chopped
2 habanero chiles, seeds and stems removed and minced
3 garlic cloves, minced
1 tablespoon brown sugar
1 tablespoon dried thyme
½ tablespoon dried ginger

Directions:

1. Combine all the ingredients in a bowl and marinate the chicken drumsticks the night before you plan to cook this recipe.
2. When you're ready to cook, preheat your air fryer to 390 degrees F.
3. Place the drumsticks in the fryer and cook for 10 minutes.
4. Lower the heat to 350 degrees F and cook for another 10 minutes. You should have a crispy and caramelized exterior on your chicken.
5. This recipe can be served with rice, noodles, corn on the cob, or salad.

Coconut-Crusted Turkey Breast

Yield: 2 servings

Ingredients:

¼ cups coconut flakes

¾ pound turkey breast, cut in half

¼ cup cornstarch

Salt and pepper to taste

1 egg, beaten

Directions:

1. Preheat your air fryer to 350 degrees F.
2. In a bowl, combine the cornstarch with some salt and pepper.
3. Dip the turkey in cornstarch first, then in eggs, and finally coat it with coconut.
4. Grease the bottom of the air fryer with cooking spray and place the coated turkey inside.
5. Cook for 10 minutes.
6. Flip over and cook for another 8 minutes.
7. Serve and enjoy!

CHAPTER SIX

Meats

Beef Burgers

Yield: 4 servings

Ingredients:

1 pound ground beef
1 small onion, diced
1 clove garlic, minced
1 teaspoon tomato paste
1 teaspoon brown mustard
2 teaspoons Italian seasoning
4 slices of any cheese
4 hamburger buns
Salt and pepper to taste

Directions:

1. Preheat air fryer to 390 degrees F.
2. In a bowl, combine the ground beef with the onion, garlic, tomato, mustard, seasonings, and salt and pepper by hand.
3. Once mixed, form into four patties and place in the fryer pan.
4. Cook in the air fryer for 15 minutes. Check them and flip, and cook for another 15 minutes.
5. Serve them on buns with your favorite condiments and side salads.

Asian Steak

Yield: 4 servings

Ingredients:

1 pound steak
1 cup cilantro leaves, finely chopped
¼ cup mint leaves, finely chopped
2 tablespoons oregano leaves, finely chopped
3 garlic cloves, finely chopped
1 teaspoon red pepper powder
1 tablespoon cumin powder
1 teaspoon cayenne pepper powder
2 teaspoons smoked paprika powder
Salt to taste
¼ teaspoon black pepper
1 tablespoon olive oil
3 tablespoons red wine vinegar

Directions:

1. Add cilantro leaves, mint leaves, oregano leaves, cloves, pepper powder, cumin powder, cayenne pepper, paprika, salt, and pepper to a bowl along with oil and vinegar, and mix until well combined.
2. Cut steak into small pieces. Add steak to herb mixture and marinate for 2 to 24 hours in fridge.
3. Preheat air fryer to 390 degrees F.
4. Pat steak dry using tissues. Place in basket and fry for 10 to 12 minutes or until desired doneness.
5. Serve with sauce of your choice.

Beef Empanadas

Yield: 4 servings

Ingredients:

1 pound ground beef
1 onion, diced
2 garlic cloves, minced
½ bell pepper, diced
¼ cup salsa
¼ teaspoon cumin
¼ cup milk
1 egg yolk
4 empanada shells
Salt and pepper to taste

Directions:

1. Brown the ground beef, onion, and garlic in a skillet for 8 minutes.
2. Drain any excess fat and add the bell pepper, salsa, and cumin.
3. Continue browning for 5 minutes.
4. Whisk the milk and egg yolk to make an egg wash.
5. Lay out the empanada shells on a counter.
6. Fill with the meat and fold the dough over.
7. Preheat the air fryer to 350 degrees F.
8. Brush the empanadas with the egg wash and place into air fryer.
9. Cook for 10 minutes.

Beef & Broccoli

Yield: 4 servings

Ingredients:

¾ pound round steak
⅓ cup oyster sauce
¼ cup sherry
2 tablespoon sesame oil
1 tablespoon soy sauce
1 tablespoon sugar
1 tablespoon cornstarch
1 pound broccoli (use only the florets)
1 garlic clove, minced
1 tablespoon minced ginger
1 tablespoon olive oil

Directions:

1. Cut the steak into thin strips.
2. In a bowl, blend the oyster sauce, sherry, sesame oil, soy sauce, sugar, and cornstarch.
3. Marinate beef strips in the mixture for 1 hour.
4. Preheat air fryer to 360 degrees F.
5. Place the marinated beef, broccoli, garlic, and ginger in the air fryer.
6. Drizzle with the olive oil and cook for 12 minutes.
7. Serve over rice.

Cheeseburger with Everything

Yield: 2 servings

Ingredients:

1 pound ground beef

2 slices Swiss or American cheese

4 bacon strips (optional)

2 hamburger buns

4 onion slices

4 tomato slices

Lettuce leaves

Condiments

Directions:

1. Heat the air fryer to 360 degrees F.
2. Shape the ground beef into 2 patties.
3. Place patties and the bacon into the basket of the air fryer. Cook for 8 minutes.
4. Top the hamburger patties with cheese and onions.
5. Place the sliced buns on top of the burgers.
6. Continue cooking for 3 minutes.
7. Add tomato slices, lettuce, and desired condiments.

Worcestershire Meatloaf

Yield: 2 servings

Ingredients:

¼ onion, diced
¾ pound ground beef
¼ cup breadcrumbs
1 tablespoon ketchup
1 tablespoon Worcestershire sauce
1 teaspoon sugar
1 teaspoon Italian seasoning
¼ teaspoon garlic salt
Pinch of pepper
¼ teaspoon paprika

Directions:

1. Preheat your air fryer to 350 degrees F.
2. Place all of the ingredients in a large bowl.
3. Mix with your hand until fully incorporated.
4. Grease a loaf pan with some cooking spray or oil. Press the beef mixture into it.
5. Place the loaf pan in the air fryer.
6. Cook for 25 minutes.
7. Serve and enjoy!

Pork Casserole

Yield: 6 servings
Ingredients:
1 cup uncooked white rice
3 cups water
3 slices bacon
2 pounds ground pork
1 tablespoon butter
1 medium red onion, chopped
¼ cup celery, chopped
¼ cup flour
2 cups milk
½ cup mushrooms
½ cup tomatoes
2 tablespoons fresh parsley, chopped
Salt and pepper to taste
½ cup mozzarella cheese

Directions:

1. Add water to a saucepan and bring to a boil. Add rice and allow it to cook.
2. Add butter to a pan along with onion and celery and cook until brown.
3. Add pork meat and milk and mix until well combined.
4. Toss in mushrooms, tomatoes, flour, salt, and pepper and mix until well combined. Bring to a boil and reduce heat.
5. When rice is cooked, add to pan and mix.
6. Preheat air fryer to 390 degrees F.
7. Add pork mixture to a dish and place bacon slices on top.
8. Sprinkle with cheese and bake for 15 to 20 minutes or until cheese melts and browns.
9. Serve warm.

Pork Empanadas

Yield: 5 servings

Ingredients:

2 tablespoons olive oil
1 pound ground pork meat
1 red onion, chopped
1½ cups pumpkin purée
3 tablespoons water
1 red chili pepper, chopped
½ teaspoon cinnamon powder
½ teaspoon dried thyme
Salt and pepper to taste
1 package of 10 empanada discs

Directions:

1. Heat a pan over medium-high heat and add oil. Toss in onion and brown.
2. Add pork meat, pumpkin puree, and water and mix well.
3. Add chili, cinnamon, thyme, salt, and pepper and mix well. Allow to thicken a little.
4. Meanwhile, line empanada discs on a plate. Fill with pork filling and close edges using fork.
5. Brush olive oil on empanadas.
6. Preheat air fryer to 390 degrees F.
7. Add empanadas and fry at 360 degrees F for 3 to 4 minutes or until crispy.
8. Serve hot, with sauce of your choice.

Pork Chops

Yield: 2 servings

Ingredients:

2 pork chops

Salt and pepper to taste

⅓ cup flour

1 large egg, beaten

½ cup panko breadcrumbs

1 tablespoon olive oil

Directions:

1. Preheat air fryer to 350 degrees F.
2. Season the pork chops with salt and pepper.
3. Place the flour, egg, and breadcrumbs in three separate shallow bowls.
4. Coat the chops with the flour, then dip in the egg, and then press into the crumbs.
5. Drizzle a little oil over the chops.
6. Place pork chops in the air fryer, and cook for 12 minutes.

Barbeque Pork

Yield: 4 servings

Ingredients:

4 pieces of pork loin (6-8 ounces each)
2 tablespoons balsamic vinegar
1 tablespoon soy sauce
2 tablespoons honey
1 clove garlic, minced
1 teaspoon fresh ginger, grated
Salt and pepper to taste

Directions:

1. Season the pork with salt and pepper.
2. Put the vinegar, soy sauce, honey, and garlic in a bowl and whisk. Add the ginger and marinate the pork for 30 minutes.
3. Preheat your air fryer to 350 degrees F.
4. Cook the pork on the baking tray of your fryer for 8 minutes and then flip them to cook on the other side for another 8 minutes.
5. Serve with baked beans or slaw.

Pigs in Blankets

Yield: 2 servings

Ingredients:

20 mini hot dogs or Vienna sausages

10 Strips of refrigerated puff pastry, cut in half

¼ cup barbeque sauce

Directions:

1. Preheat your air fryer to 390 degrees F.
2. Spread each strip of pastry with barbeque sauce.
3. Wrap the strips of pastry around the hot dogs securely.
4. Place them in the air fryer basket and cook for 10 minutes (two batches may be necessary).
5. Serve with extra barbeque sauce.

Middle Eastern Meatballs

Yield: 6 servings

Ingredients:

1 pound ground lamb
4 ounces ground chicken
1½ tablespoons cilantro, finely chopped
1 tablespoon mint, finely chopped
1 teaspoon cumin powder
1 teaspoon coriander powder
1 teaspoon cayenne pepper powder
1 teaspoon red chili paste
2 garlic cloves, finely chopped
¼ cup olive oil
1 teaspoon salt
1 egg white

Directions:

1. Preheat air fryer to 390 degrees F.
2. Add lamb, chicken, cilantro, mint, cumin, coriander, cayenne, red chili, and garlic to a bowl and mix until well combined.
3. Add egg whites to a bowl along with salt and mix well. Pour this into meat mixture and combine into dough.
4. Roll out small balls from mixture.
5. Apply some oil on surface of meatballs and place in the basket.
6. Lower heat to 360 degrees F and cook meatballs for 6 to 8 minutes or until golden on all sides.
7. Serve with mint chutney.

Sausage and Peppers

Yield: 3 servings

Ingredients:

6 Italian sausages (hot or sweet)

1 red bell pepper, sliced into strips

1 green bell pepper, sliced into strips

1 small red onion, cut into chunks

1 package sauerkraut (16 ounces)

¼ cup mustard

Directions:

1. Preheat your air fryer to 350 degrees F.

2. Cut up the pepper and onion strips and set aside.

3. Arrange the sausages in the air fryer basket and cook for 5 minutes. Give them a toss to ensure browning on all sides and prevent sticking, and cover with the peppers and onions. Cook for another 5 minutes.

4. Serve with the sauerkraut and mustard, or put them into hoagie rolls for sausage sandwiches.

CHAPTER SEVEN

Fish and Seafood

Coconut Shrimp

Yield: 4 servings

Ingredients:

1 pound shrimp, peeled and deveined
½ cup flour
2 egg whites, beaten
½ cup panko breadcrumbs
½ cup coconut, shredded
1 teaspoon lime juice
½ teaspoon salt
Duck sauce

Directions:

1. Set 3 plates on the counter. Fill the plates respectively with the flour, eggs whites and breadcrumbs.
2. Blend the salt with the flour.
3. Beat the egg whites until stiff.
4. Blend the coconut and lime juice with the breadcrumbs.
5. Preheat air fryer to 390 degrees F.
6. Coat each shrimp with the flour, then dip in the egg whites, and then press into the breadcrumb mixture. Make sure all sides of the shrimps are coated.
7. Coat fryer basket with a non-stick cooking spray. Cook the shrimp in batches for 6 minutes.
8. When all the shrimp are fried, add all of them to the basket and cook at 350 degrees F for another 2 minutes.
9. Serve with duck sauce.

Fish Sticks

Yield: 4 servings

Ingredients:

1 large egg

¾ teaspoon Cajun seasoning

1 pound cod

1½ cups whole wheat flour

Salt and pepper to taste

Directions:

1. Spray the bottom of the air fryer with cooking spray.
2. Pat the fish dry. Cut into 1" stripes.
3. In a bowl, whisk the egg.
4. In a large bowl, combine the whole wheat flour, Cajun seasoning, salt, and pepper.
5. Dip each fish stick into the egg and then into the flour mixture. Toss well to cover. Place into the air fryer basket.
6. Set the temperature of the air fry at 400 degrees F and cook for 5 minutes.
7. Flip the fish sticks with a set of tongs. Cook for another 5 minutes or until golden.
8. Serve immediately.

Salmon with Dill Sauce

Yield: 4 servings

Ingredients:

For the Salmon:

2 salmon fillets

1 teaspoon olive oil

Salt to taste

For the Dill Sauce:

½ cup yogurt (non-fat)

¼ cup sour cream

Salt to taste

1 tablespoon dill, finely chopped

Directions:

1. Preheat air fryer to 250 degrees F.
2. Cut salmon into four portions. Pour a little olive oil onto each portion and sprinkle with salt.
3. Place seasoned salmon in basket and cook for 30 minutes.
4. While salmon is cooking, mix ingredients for dill sauce in a bowl.
5. When salmon is fully cooked, top salmon with sauce and serve warm.

Tuna Patties

Yield: 4 servings

Ingredients:

2 cans tuna in water

1 teaspoon Dijon mustard

½ cup panko breadcrumbs

2 tablespoons chopped parsley

1 tablespoon lemon juice

Dash of Tabasco or hot sauce

1 large egg

Salt and pepper to taste.

Directions:

1. Drain the liquid from the tuna and flake with a fork.
2. In a bowl, combine the tuna, mustard, breadcrumbs, parsley, lemon juice, and Tabasco sauce.
3. Add the egg and season with salt and pepper. Mix thoroughly.
4. Form 8 patties and refrigerate them overnight.
5. Preheat the air fryer to 360 degrees F.
6. Place the patties in the air fryer, spray with a non-stick cooking spray, and cook for 10 minutes. (For extra crispiness, cook an extra 3–4 minutes.)
7. Drizzle patties with lemon juice and serve.

Tuna Croquettes

Yield: 2 servings

Ingredients:

2 cans of tuna, drained

2 eggs, beaten

¼ cup breadcrumbs

⅓ cup vegetable oil

2 tablespoons dried parsley

Salt and pepper

Directions:

1. Preheat air fryer to 390 degrees F.
2. Mix the tuna with the eggs, oil, parsley, salt, and pepper. Roll the mixture into balls and coat them with the breadcrumbs.
3. Place them in the fryer basket and cook for 8 minutes.

Fried Shrimp

Yield: 4 servings

Ingredients:

20 tiger shrimps

¼ teaspoon cayenne pepper

½ teaspoon old bay seasoning

¼ teaspoon smoked paprika

Salt and pepper to taste

1 tablespoon olive oil

Directions:

1. Add shrimp, cayenne, seasoning, paprika, salt, and pepper to a bowl and mix until well combined.
2. Marinate in fridge for 5 to 12 hours.
3. Preheat air fryer to 390 degrees F.
4. Add shrimp to basket and fry for 10 to 15 minutes or until crispy.
5. Serve warm, with a sauce of your choice.

Shrimp, Cajun Style

Yield: 4 servings

Ingredient:

16 tiger shrimps

½ teaspoon cayenne pepper

1 teaspoon old bay seasoning

½ teaspoon smoked paprika

¼ teaspoon salt

½ tablespoon olive oil

Directions:

1. Preheat air fryer to 390 degrees F.
2. Combine all ingredients in a bowl.
3. Place shrimp in basket and cook for 10 minutes.
4. Serve as topping for rice.

Popcorn Shrimp

Yield: 2 servings

Ingredients:

24 medium uncooked white shrimps

1 cup flour

1 cup panko breadcrumbs

1 cup dried, unsweetened coconut

1 tablespoon cornstarch

4 egg whites

Directions:

1. Preheat air fryer to 350 degrees F.
2. Rinse and dry shrimp.
3. In two separate bowls, mix the breadcrumbs and the coconut and then the flour and the cornstarch.
4. Dip one shrimp at a time into the flour mixture, the egg whites, and then the coconut.
5. Place in basket and cook for 10 minutes. Check the shrimp and turn or shake.
6. Cook another 5 minutes.

Bacon Wrapped Shrimp

Yield: 5 servings

Ingredients:

10 pieces tiger shrimp (deveined)

10 slices bacon

Directions:

1. Wrap one slice of bacon around each shrimp, from the head of the shrimp to the tail.
2. Leave wrapped shrimp in fridge for 30 minutes.
3. Preheat air fryer to 390 degrees F.
4. Add shrimp to basket and cook for 10 minutes.
5. Drain shrimp of excess fat due to bacon.

Cajun Shrimp

Yield: 2 servings

Ingredients:

16 large shrimps, peeled and deveined

1 tablespoon celery salt

¼ teaspoon cayenne pepper

¼ teaspoon paprika

Dash of dry mustard

Dash of cinnamon

Salt and pepper to taste

1 tablespoon olive oil

Directions:

1. Preheat air fryer to 380 degrees F.
2. In a bowl, mix all of the spices and the oil.
3. Coat the shrimp thoroughly with the spice mix.
4. Cook the shrimp for 5 minutes.
5. Serve with rice.

Crab Cakes

Yield: 10 servings

Ingredients:

4 cups crab meat

12 Ritz crackers

1 large egg

1 onion, chopped

1 scallion, chopped

1 tablespoon corn flour

1 tablespoon mayonnaise

½ teaspoon garlic powder

Salt and pepper to taste

Directions:

1. Mix all the ingredients together in a bowl and shape into 10 patties.
2. Preheat the air fryer to 360 degrees F.
3. Add crab cake patties to basket and cook for 10 minutes.

Lemon Dill Salmon

Yield: 2 servings

Ingredients:

2 pieces of salmon (6-8 ounces each)

2 tablespoons fresh dill

1 lemon, juiced

1 teaspoon garlic powder

Salt and pepper to taste

Directions:

1. Preheat the air fryer to 350 degrees F.
2. Rinse salmon and pat dry. Season with salt and pepper.
3. In a bowl, combine the lemon juice, dill, and garlic powder. Pour over the salmon and lightly rub the liquid into the fish.
4. Place the fish on the grill pan of the fryer and cook for 8 minutes.
5. Serve over rice or pasta, or with a large salad.

CHAPTER EIGHT

Vegetables

Roasted Mushrooms

Yield: 4 servings

Ingredients:

1 pound mushrooms

2 tablespoons vegetable oil

1 teaspoon garlic, minced

1 tablespoon mixed herbs

Salt and pepper to taste

Directions:

1. Wash and cut mushrooms into halves.
2. Add to a bowl along with oil, garlic, herbs, salt, and pepper and mix until well combined.
3. Add to air fryer and roast for 10 to 15 minutes or until crispy.
4. Serve hot, with sauce of your choice.

Cheesy Asparagus

Yield: 4 servings

Ingredients:

½ cup grated parmesan cheese

2 tablespoons Italian seasoning

½ cup heavy cream

1 pound asparagus

Salt and pepper to taste

Directions:

1. Preheat the air fryer to 400 degrees F.
2. Remove the stems from the asparagus.
3. Whisk together the heavy cream, Italian seasoning, and parmesan cheese.
4. Place the asparagus in a dish. Cover with the cream mixture.
5. Place the dish in the air fryer and cook for 8 minutes.
6. Sprinkle the asparagus with salt and pepper before serving.

Grilled Corn

Yield: 2 servings

Ingredients:

2 whole corn-on-the-cobs

2 tablespoons grated feta cheese

2 teaspoons paprika

1 teaspoon olive oil

Directions:

1. Preheat the air fryer to 400 degrees F.
2. Discard the silks and husks from each ear of corn.
3. Grease the corns with olive oil and give them a sprinkle of paprika.
4. Cook in the air fryer for 15 minutes.
5. Place the corns on a serving dish with the cheese as a topping.

Cauliflower Fritters

Yield: 6 servings

Ingredients:

1 large cauliflower

1 tablespoon chili powder

½ teaspoon turmeric powder

Salt to taste

2 tablespoons vegetable oil

Directions:

1. Boil the cauliflower and separate it into florets.
2. Add it to a bowl along with chili powder, turmeric, and salt, and mix until well combined. Allow it to stand for 1o minutes.
3. Preheat air fryer to 390 degrees F.
4. Brush oil over the cauliflower and add to the basket.
5. Fry for 10 to 15 minutes or until crispy.
6. Serve hot, with a sauce of your choice.

Asparagus Salad

Yield: 4 servings

Ingredients:

10 ounces white asparagus
8 ounces green asparagus
1 cup chicory
4 boiled eggs
10 ounces boiled potatoes
10 ounces ham, cubed
6 small radishes, sliced
6 cherry tomatoes, halved
Lettuce leaves
1 tablespoon olive oil

Directions:

1. Remove the stems from the asparagus and cut into bite-sized pieces.
2. Insert a dish in the air fryer.
3. Preheat to 380 degrees F and add the olive oil.
4. Add asparagus, ham, and potatoes and cook for 10 minutes.
5. Remove the dish from the air fryer and let cool.
6. Stir in the radishes and tomatoes. Add salt and pepper to taste.
7. Chop the eggs and add to asparagus mix.
8. Lay the lettuce and chicory on a large plate and top with the asparagus mix. Serve warm.

Roasted Vegetables

Yield: 4 servings

Ingredients:

1 cup potato, chopped

1 cup celery stalks, chopped

2 red onions, chopped

1 butternut squash, chopped

1 tablespoon fresh thyme leaves

1 tablespoon olive oil

Salt and pepper to taste

Directions:

1. Preheat air fryer to 390 degrees F.
2. Add potatoes, celery, onion, squash, pepper, salt, and thyme to a bowl and mix until well combined.
3. Add in oil and toss.
4. Add vegetables to basket and fry for 10 minutes.
5. Serve hot.

Vegetable Dumplings

Yield: 5 servings

Ingredients:

For the Stuffing:

2 cups cabbage, shredded
1 carrot, chopped
2 large onions, chopped
1 green pepper
1 2-inch slice ginger
8 garlic cloves, chopped
Salt and pepper to taste
1 tablespoon soy sauce
1 tablespoon olive oil
1 scallion

For the Rolls:

10 spring roll sheets
2 tablespoons corn flour or plain flour
Water

Directions:

1. Preheat air fryer to 390 degrees F.
2. Add oil to a pan along with onions and garlic and sauté.
3. Add green pepper, cabbage, and ginger and sauté till brown.
4. Add salt, pepper, and soy sauce and mix until well combined.
5. Add scallion last and mix.
6. Lay spring roll sheet on a plate and add about 2 tbsp. of filling.
7. Make a paste using flour and water. Use a finger to apply the paste on the edges of the spring roll sheet. Roll sheet to seal the filling in.
8. Add to fryer and fry for 20 minutes or until crispy.
9. Serve warm, with noodles and a sauce of your choice.

Vegetable and Chickpea Balls

Yield: 4 servings

Ingredients:

1 cup chickpeas

1 cup mixed vegetables (corn, carrots, beans, and peas)

½ cup breadcrumbs

1 teaspoon cumin powder

1 teaspoon all spice powder

1 tablespoon cilantro leaves

1 teaspoon red chili powder

1 tablespoon cornstarch powder

Salt to taste

Directions:

1. Preheat air fryer to 360 degrees F.
2. Boil vegetables and chickpeas until soft. Add to bowl and mash.
3. Toss in cumin powder, all spice powder, cilantro leaves, red chili powder, and cornstarch and mix together.
4. Make small balls out of mixture.
5. Place breadcrumbs on a plate. Roll balls on it and place in basket.
6. Fry for 5 minutes at 300 degrees F.
7. Serve hot, with sauce of your choice.

Roasted Carrots

Yield: 2 servings

Ingredients:

1 cup carrots, split in half

Olive oil to brush

4 tablespoons honey

Salt and pepper to taste

Directions:

1. Add carrots to a bowl along with honey, oil, salt, and pepper and marinate for 2 to 3 hours.
2. Preheat air fryer to 390 degrees F.
3. Add carrots and fry for 10 to 12 minutes.
4. Serve warm.

Crispy Brussels Sprouts

Yield: 4 servings
Ingredients:
1 pound Brussels sprouts
5 teaspoons olive oil
½ teaspoon kosher salt

Directions:

1. Preheat air fryer to 390 degrees F.
2. Add sprouts to a bowl along with oil and salt and mix until well combined.
3. Place in fryer to fry 15 to 20 minutes or until crispy.
4. Serve hot.

Baked Potatoes

Yield: 6 servings

Ingredients:

3 large potatoes
2 tablespoons olive oil
1 teaspoon salt
1 tablespoon garlic, minced
1 teaspoon parsley leaves
1 teaspoon rosemary leaves

Directions:

1. Preheat air fryer to 390 degrees F.
2. Scrub potatoes and poke holes in them using a fork.
3. Add to a bowl along with oil, salt, garlic, parsley, and rosemary leaves and rub well until fully coated.
4. Add potatoes to fryer and fry for 12 to 15 minutes or until crispy.
5. Serve warm.

Baked Spud

Yield: 4 servings
Ingredients:
4 russet potatoes
2 green onions, chopped
½ cup sour cream
¼ cup fresh chives, chopped
Salt and pepper to taste

Directions:

1. Preheat air fryer to 400 degrees F.
2. Wash and dry potatoes. Place them in the basket and cook for 20 minutes.
3. Stir the chives and onions into the sour cream.
4. When the potatoes are ready, slice them lengthwise and cover with the sour cream mixture.

Roasted Parsnip, Celery, and Squash

Yield: 4 servings

Ingredients:

1 parsnip

3 stalks celery

2 small red onions

1 butternut squash

½ tablespoon fresh thyme

½ tablespoon olive oil

Salt and pepper to taste

Directions:

1. Preheat air fryer to 300 degrees F.
2. Peel and cut onions into wedges. Peel parsnip and cut it and celery stalks into cubes of 2 cm each.
3. De-seed butternut squash and cut into cubes.
4. Mix cut vegetables with olive oil and thyme and season.
5. Place seasoned vegetables in basket and roast in the air fryer for 20 minutes. Mix vegetables once after 10 minutes.
6. When timer goes off, check vegetables to see if they have turned brown.
7. Serve hot.

CHAPTER NINE

Dessert

Carrot Cake

Yield: 6 servings

Ingredients:

2 cups flour
2 teaspoons baking soda
1 teaspoon cinnamon
½ teaspoon salt
½ cup honey
½ cup canola oil
½ cup applesauce
¼ cup plain yogurt
3 large eggs
2 teaspoons vanilla
2 carrots, shredded
½ cup raisins
½ cup walnuts

For the Frosting:

1 cup cream cheese, softened
1 cup powdered sugar
½ cup plain yogurt
1 teaspoon vanilla
1 teaspoon lemon juice
¼ teaspoon milk ONLY if needed to soften icing.

Directions:

1. Spray the baking tray with a non-stick cooking spray.

2. In a bowl, sift together the flour, baking soda, cinnamon, and salt. Set aside.

3. In a mixer with a bowl, whip together the honey and the oil. Add the applesauce and the yogurt.

4. Add 1 egg at a time, whipping the mixture well after each egg. Add the vanilla.

5. Preheat the air fryer to 350 degrees F.

6. Use a spatula to blend the wet ingredients into the dry mixture.

7. Gently mix in the shredded carrots, raisins, and walnuts.

8. Pour the batter into the baking tray and place in the air fryer. Cover the tray with foil.

9. Bake for 30 minutes.

10. Remove the carrot cake and let cool.

11. For the frosting, use a food processer to soften the cream cheese.

12. Add the powdered sugar and blend until smooth.

13. Add the yogurt, vanilla, and lemon juice and blend further. Let the frosting thicken in the refrigerator for a few hours.

14. Frost the carrot cake and top with walnuts.

Chocolate Cake

Yield: 8 servings
Ingredients:
3 medium eggs
½ cup sour cream
1 cup flour
2/3 cup sugar
9 tablespoons butter
6 tablespoons cocoa powder
1 teaspoon baking powder
½ teaspoon baking soda
2 teaspoons vanilla extract

For the Chocolate icing:
5½ ounces chocolate
3½ tablespoons softened butter
2 cups icing sugar
1 teaspoon vanilla extract

Directions:

1. Preheat air fryer to 320 degrees F.
2. Add eggs to a bowl along with vanilla extract, cream, sugar, and butter and beat until well combined.
3. Sieve flour, cocoa powder, baking powder, and baking soda and add to wet ingredients.
4. Mix until well combined.
5. Add batter to baking dish and place in air fryer (will fit in an 8 inch tin).
6. Bake for 35 minutes. Use a skewer or toothpick to check if it is done.
7. If it is not done, allow it to cook for a further 5 minutes.
8. Meanwhile, prepare icing by melting chocolate in double boiler.

9. Add in butter, sugar, and vanilla and mix until well combined.

10. Pour over cake and wait for it to harden a little before serving.

Blueberry Crumble

Yield: 6 servings

Ingredients:

18 ounces fresh blueberries

6 ounces fresh blackberries

½ cup sugar

2 tablespoons lemon juice

1 cup flour

Salt

5 tablespoons butter

Directions:

1. Preheat air fryer to 390 degrees F.
2. Add blueberries, blackberries, lemon juice, and sugar to a bowl and mix until well combined.
3. Add flour, salt, and butter to a bowl and use fingers to crumble it together.
4. Add berries to a baking dish and add crumble on top.
5. Press down gently and place in air fryer.
6. Bake for 20 minutes at 390 degrees F.
7. Serve hot.

Banana Split

Yield: 4 servings

Ingredients:

4 ripe bananas
2 tablespoons butter, softened
2 eggs
½ cup flour
1 cup bread crumbs
2 tablespoons cinnamon
1 tablespoon sugar
4 cups ice cream
1 cup whipped cream
4 cherries

Directions:

1. Preheat the air fryer to 300 degrees F.
2. Combine the butter and the bread crumbs with a fork.
3. Cut the bananas in half and roll them in the flour, then the eggs, then the bread crumb mixture. Place side by side in the air fryer.
4. Cook for 10 minutes.
5. Remove the bananas and sprinkle with cinnamon and sugar.
6. Place two halves in a dish and cover with ice cream, whipped cream, and a cherry.

Apple Pie Packets

Yield: 10 servings

Ingredients:

3 medium apples, sliced and chopped into small pieces

½ cup butter, melted

2 teaspoons flour

2 teaspoons brown sugar

1 tablespoon lemon juice

1 tablespoon cinnamon

1 teaspoon nutmeg

1 teaspoon allspice

10 sheets filo pastry

Directions:

1. Preheat air fryer to 325 degrees F.
2. In a bowl, combine the apples, lemon juice, flour, sugars, cinnamon, nutmeg, and allspice.
3. Unroll the filo pastry onto a clean surface. Keep this dough from drying out by laying damp paper towels over it.
4. Brush the pastry with butter. Place a scoop of the apple filling in the center of the pastry. Fold the bottom of the pastry sheet up over the filling. Continue folding as if you are folding a towel or a flag. Brush with butter occasionally.
5. Complete a triangle that is folded on the ends, and brush the entire pouch with melted butter.
6. Cook in the fryer for 8 minutes.
7. Cool before serving.

Candied Lemons

Yield: 4 servings

Ingredients:

2 organic lemons without wax on the skins

½ cup sugar

¼ cup boiling water

Directions:

1. Preheat air fryer to 300 degrees F.
2. Pour sugar into a small bowl and add the boiling water. Stir until dissolved.
3. Slice lemons thinly and dip them into the sugar water mix.
4. Cook them in the fryer for about 15–20 minutes. They should be slightly sticky.
5. Serve with ice cream or pudding.

Chocolate Brownies with Caramel Sauce

Yield: 6 servings

Ingredients:

4 tablespoons unsalted butter

8 ounces semi-sweet chocolate

2 large eggs

1 cup powdered sugar

¾ cup sugar

½ teaspoon salt

1 cup baking flour

1 teaspoon vanilla

Directions:

1. Preheat the air fryer to 350 degrees F.
2. Using a microwave or double boiler, melt 2 tablespoons of the butter with the chocolate.
3. Mix in the sugar, eggs, and vanilla and blend well.
4. Add the flour and mix thoroughly.
5. Transfer the mixture into a baking dish and place into the air fryer. Cook for 15 minutes.
6. For the caramel sauce, blend the powdered sugar with 1½ tablespoons water in a small pan. Let the sugar melt over medium-low heat.
7. Remove the sauce from the stove and mix in the remaining 2 tablespoons butter.
8. When the butter is melted, stir in the milk. Let cool.
9. Remove the brownies from the air fryer. Once cooled, cut them into squares and serve with the caramel sauce.

Vanilla Soufflé

Yield: 6 servings

Ingredients:

¼ cup all-purpose flour
¼ cup butter, softened
1 cup whole milk
¼ cup sugar
2 teaspoons vanilla extract
5 egg whites
4 egg yolks
1 ounce sugar
1 teaspoon cream of tartar

Directions:

1. Preheat air fryer to 330 degrees F.
2. Add milk to a pan and add in sugar. Heat pan over medium heat to dissolve sugar.
3. Add egg whites, sugar, and cream of tartar to a bowl. Beat until fluffy and peaks form.
4. Add egg yolks and vanilla to another bowl and beat until well combined.
5. Line 6 ramekins with butter.
6. Mix yellow mixture into white mixture gently, so as not to deflate peaks.
7. Add in milk and mix gently.
8. Pour mix into ramekins and place in air fryer.
9. Bake for 14 to 15 minutes or until done.
10. Serve warm.

Chocolate Soufflés

Yield: 4 servings

Ingredients:

3 ounces semi-sweet chocolate, chopped

¼ cup butter, plus 2 teaspoons for the ramekins

2 large eggs, separated

4 tablespoons sugar

½ teaspoon vanilla

2 tablespoons flour

Powdered sugar for dusting

Heavy cream

Directions:

1. Butter two ramekins and sprinkle with sugar.
2. Using a double boiler or a microwave, melt the chocolate with the ¼ cup butter.
3. In a bowl, whisk the eggs yolks, sugar, and vanilla.
4. Very slowly, add the melted chocolate mixture while stirring.
5. Add the flour and stir until the batter is smooth.
6. Preheat the air fryer to 330 degrees F.
7. In another bowl, beat the egg whites to a peak and gently fold into the batter.
8. Divide the batter between the prepared ramekins. Leave a bit of room on top.
9. Transfer the ramekins to the air fryer and cook for 14 minutes.
10. Remove the soufflés from the air fryer, dust with the powdered sugar and serve hot with the heavy cream.

Glazed Donuts

Yield: 8 servings

Ingredients:

1 can prepared biscuit dough

¼ cup milk

2 cups powdered sugar

Directions:

1. Preheat the air fryer to 390 degrees F.
2. For the glaze, combine the milk and the sugar. Let the sugar dissolve and set aside.
3. Use a cookie cutter or shot glass to poke a hole in the biscuit.
4. Spray the bottom of the air fryer with non-stick cooking spray and insert the donuts.
5. Air fry for 5 minutes.
6. Remove the donuts from the air fryer, and drop each donut in the glaze.
7. Let sit for a few minutes. Add sprinkles if desired.

Baked Pears

Yield: 2 servings

Ingredients:

2 pears

2 tablespoons raisins

2 tablespoons milk

1 tablespoon cinnamon

2 sheets fresh puff pastry dough (ready to use)

Directions:

1. Preheat air fryer to 350 degrees F.

2. Peel and core the pears. Slice them in half and scoop out some extra fruit to make a small hole in each side. Mix the fruit with the raisins and the cinnamon. Fill the holes in 2 of the pear halves with that mixture.

3. Place one pear half on a sheet of pastry and cover it with the corresponding (and empty) pear half so it looks like one whole pear again. Wrap in the pastry and tuck in or fold the ends. Brush with milk. Do the same thing with the other pear halves.

4. Cook for 20 minutes.

Victoria Sponge

Yield: 6 servings

Ingredients:

1 cup plain flour

1 cup butter, melted

1 cup sugar

2 medium eggs

For the Filling:

2 tablespoons strawberry jam

½ cup butter

1 cup icing sugar

1 tablespoon whipped cream

Directions:

1. Preheat air fryer to 390 degrees F.
2. Add butter and sugar to a bowl and beat until light and fluffy.
3. Beat eggs in another bowl to form stiff peaks. Mix eggs with butter and fold gently.
4. Add in flour and mix until well combined. Add to greased bowl and place in air fryer.
5. Bake for 20 to 25 minutes at 390 degrees F. Use a skewer to check whether the cake is done.
6. Add jam, butter, sugar, and cream to a bowl.
7. Cut cake in half and apply cream in between layers.
8. Sandwich the other half on top and serve.

Banana Cake

Yield: 6 servings

Ingredients:

½ cup butter, softened

⅓ cup brown sugar

1 medium egg

1 banana, mashed

2 tablespoons honey

1 cup self-rising flour

½ teaspoon cinnamon powder

1 teaspoon salt

Directions:

1. Add butter to bowl along with sugar and cinnamon and beat until well combined and fluffy.
2. Beat egg in a separate bowl until fluffy and light. Combine the two.
3. Add in mashed banana and fold into mixture.
4. Sieve dry ingredients, and mix with wet ingredients until well combined.
5. Preheat air fryer to 390 degrees F.
6. Add cake mixture to baking bowl, place in fryer, and bake for 30 minutes.
7. Serve warm.

Cinnamon Rolls

Yield: 8 servings
Ingredients:
1 pound bread dough
¼ cup butter, melted
1 cup brown sugar
1½ tablespoons cinnamon

For the cream cheese frosting:
4 oz. cream cheese, softened
2 tablespoons softened butter
1 cup powdered sugar
½ teaspoon vanilla

Directions:

1. If the dough is frozen, thaw to room temperature.
2. On a floured surface, roll out the dough into a rectangle.
3. Brush the dough with the melted butter.
4. Combine the brown sugar and cinnamon in a small bowl.
5. Spoon the sugar mixture over the dough.
6. Roll the dough tightly into a log.
7. Press on the edges to seal the dough.
8. Cut the dough into 8 pieces.
9. Cover with a towel and let sit for 2 hours.
10. To prepare the frosting, soften the cream cheese and the butter in the microwave and stir.
11. Mix in the powdered sugar and the vanilla, and set aside.
12. Preheat the air fryer to 350 degrees F.
13. Place half of the rolls in the air fryer basket and fry for 5 minutes. Flip the rolls over and fry for 4 more minutes. Repeat with the remaining rolls.
14. Allow the rolls to cool.
15. Top with the frosting and serve warm.

Chocolate Chip Cookies

Yield: 9 servings

Ingredients:

4 ounces butter

3 ounces brown sugar

2 tablespoons honey

¾ cup flour

¾ cup chocolate

1½ tablespoons milk

Directions:

1. Preheat the air fryer to 360 degrees F.
2. Cream the butter and sugar until smooth.
3. Add the honey and stir; add the flour and continue stirring.
4. Use a mallet or rolling pin to break the chocolate into chunks.
5. Mix the chocolate and milk into the batter and blend well.
6. Place a baking sheet in the air fryer, and spoon the batter into the air fryer making 9 cookies.
7. Bake for 6 minutes. Reduce heat to 340 degrees F and bake another 2 minutes or until light brown.

Chocolate Chip Cupcakes

Yield: 6 servings

Ingredients:

½ cup self-rising flour
½ cup all-purpose flour
1 teaspoon salt
½ teaspoon baking soda
1 tablespoon cocoa powder
2 tablespoons plain yogurt
½ cup sugar
4 tablespoons whole milk
½ teaspoon vegetable oil
1 teaspoon apple cider
¼ cup chocolate chips
Cupcake liners

Directions:

1. Preheat air fryer to 390 degrees F.
2. Combine flours, baking soda, and salt. Add cocoa.
3. In a small bowl, combine the sugar, milk, yogurt, vanilla, and oil. Mix in the cider.
4. Combine the dry and wet ingredients and mix. Add the chocolate chips. Spoon the mixture into cupcake liners.
5. Cook them 4 at a time in the fryer for 10 minutes.
6. Add frosting or powdered sugar, or eat them just like they are.

Fruit Kabobs

Yield: 4 servings
Ingredients:
1 apple, cored and cut into chunks
1 mango, cut into chunks
1 pear, cored and cut into chunks
1 orange, peeled and divided into segments
1 teaspoon honey
1 teaspoon lemon juice
Salt to taste
¼ cup pomegranate seeds
Skewers

Directions:

1. Preheat air fryer to 350 degrees F.
2. In a bowl, combine the lemon juice and honey. Add the fruit pieces and coat with the mixture. Sprinkle with salt. Divide the fruit onto skewers and place in the fryer.
3. Cook for 5 minutes for a grilled flavor.
4. Put them on a plate and sprinkle with pomegranate seeds.

Conclusion

The air fryer is a revolutionary kitchen appliance. This book provides you with delicious and healthy air fryer recipes which you can whip up in minutes, even if you do not know how to cook. I hope you enjoy the recipes!

Finally, I want to thank you for reading my book. If you enjoyed the book, please take the time to share your thoughts and post a review on the Amazon website. It would be greatly appreciated!

Best wishes,

Savannah Gibbs

Check Out My Other Books

Spiralizer Cookbook: Easy, Delicious, and Healthy Recipes for Your Spiralizer

Fermentation for Beginners: Delicious Fermented Vegetable Recipes for Better Digestion and Health

Mediterranean Diet Cookbook: Easy and Delicious Mediterranean Diet Recipes to Lose Weight and Lower Your Risk of Heart Disease

Weight Loss Smoothies: 45 Delicious Smoothie Recipes to Lose Weight and Get Healthy

Electric Pressure Cooker Cookbook: Quick, Easy, and Healthy Electric Pressure Cooker Recipes for Your Family

CPSIA information can be obtained
at www.ICGtesting.com
Printed in the USA
LVHW080413090621
689771LV00010B/482

9 781951 548384